Traveling for
No Good Reason

Traveling for No Good Reason

poems

George Franklin

Sheila-Na-Gig Editions
Volume 2

Copyright © 2018 George Franklin

Author photo: © Ximena Gómez
Cover photo: © Ximena Gómez

ISBN: 9781732940604

Published by Sheila-Na-Gig Editions
www.sheilanagigblog.com

ALL RIGHTS RESERVED
Printed in the United States of America

DEDICATION

To *mi amor* Ximena, who inhabits all my poems, even the ones written before I knew her.

To Hadley & Toby & Simon, who are my children, my friends, and readers over my shoulder.

And to the friends who read many of the poems in this book—before it was a book—and gave me their suggestions and support: Dick Ravin, Nancy Schoenberger, and Kacee Belcher.

ACKNOWLEDGMENTS

Many thanks to the editors and staff of the following journals in which these poems have appeared:

Armarolla: "Looking Backwards," and "Palimpsest."

B O D Y: "Letting Go."

Cagibi: "On a Day in March."

Conexos: "Moving."

Gulf Stream: "Barcelona."

Matter: A (somewhat) monthly journal of political poetry and commentary: "A Conversation about Dictators," "Montage."

Pedestal Magazine: "Origami."

Rumble Fish Quarterly: "Oddly Shaped Windows."

Salamander: "Vienna, 1933-34."

Sheila-Na-Gig online: "A Steady Stream," "Between," "Cinders," "Goya," "Leaves Falling on the Roof," "Miami," "Moving," and "Rain."

The Ghazal Page: "A Demitasse," "A Phone Call," "Ghazal," "Over Coffee," and "Poem of the Street."

The Threepenny Review: "Nietzsche in Turin, 1889."

The Wild Word: "Respect," and "Speaking of Love."

Twyckenham Notes: "The Way It Is Now."

Vending Machine Press: "Pigeon Wings," "Road Trip," and "Sadness."

Special thanks to Katakana Editores for permission to publish "Moving" and "Rain," which appear in *Among the Ruins*, a bilingual collection of my poems translated by Ximena Gomez.

CONTENTS

DEDICATION	5
ACKNOWLEDGMENTS	6
Miami	11
Leaves Falling on the Roof	12
East of Shark Valley	13
The Blue Station Wagon	14
Looking Backwards	15
Between	16
The Life of Things	17
This and That	18
Black Lake	19
Scrapbooks	20
Smoke	20
A Demitasse	23
Take Solace Where You Can Find It	24
Apartment on First	25
The Rockaways	26
Memorial Drive	27
Road Trip	28
Reading the Greeks	29
Near Columbia	30
A Steady Stream	31
Rain	32
Caravaggio at the Execution of Beatrice Cenci	34
Cinders	35
Goya	36

Schopenhauer	37
Respect	38
When It's Difficult	40
Access Denied	41
In the Waiting Room	43
A Guest	45
Sadness	46
Barcelona	47
Ghazal	48
Anywhere	49
Poem of the Street	50
Moving	51
Over Coffee	52
A Friend Asks How I Write a Poem	53
Allegory of Grief	54
A Few Days Later	55
Lives of the Stars	56
The Cyclops	57
Without Footprints	58
Pigeon Wings	60
Montage	62
Phone Call	63
Oddly Shaped Windows	64
Venice Weather	65
The Way It Is Now	68
In Your Country	69
For a While	70
Letting Go	71
Chatter of Rain	73

You Joke	74
A Certain Age	75
Origami	76
A Great Emptiness	77
Nothing Dramatic	78
Frank	79
Borges Says Arranging a Library Is an Act of Criticism	81
Palimpsest	82
Baedeker's Guide to Eternity	84
Crime Scene	86
Apple Harvest	87
Mouths Pressed	88
Apology	89
Why Poetry?	91
In the Ghetto Nuovo	92
Nietzsche in Turin, 1889	93
Vienna 1933-34	94
A Conversation About Dictators	95
Robert Frost in Key West	97
Reading Cesare Pavese in Takee-Outee	98
Floorboards	100
Paradox	101
"Thus"	102
On a Day in March	103
Speaking of Love	105

I. Looking Backwards

Miami

Men in t-shirts drinking Cuban coffee
Outside a restaurant by the airport, the smell of
Roast pork and plantains, white rice and black
Beans, voices that have all known each
Other for years or sound like it, and the sun
That grows a little hotter each day of April—
Sometimes I wonder how I ended up here, a
Gringo par excellence, to mix up my languages,
No one less likely to tan on the beach or drive
A car that turns heads, no one less likely either
To smile at the pretty waitress, Afro-Cuban,
In a tight shirt and jeans. I fill a cup with
Ice water from the orange plastic cooler
On the counter and watch the planes skim over
The rooftops of warehouses on their way
To all the places I think of moving if life doesn't
Work out for me here. I tell myself there's always
Venice or some small town in Umbria,
Or a Greek island where every morning
The baker will take round loaves out of the oven
And every afternoon, fishermen will sell
Their catch on the sun-warmed sand. Everyone
Dreams of escape, but not always from the same
Thing. All I need, I think, is a café where they'll
Let me sit over espresso, read books, and write.
None of this is true, though. I need more than
I can possibly imagine. I'm hopelessly American
And awful at speaking anything but English.
I don't know even what it is I'm trying to leave.
I think of Cavafy's poem, "The City," with
Its warning that as you've wasted your life here,
You've wasted it everywhere else as well. I picture
His large eyebrows sticking out from behind his glasses,
Frowning at me, inquiring if I've learned absolutely
Nothing so far. So, I take a deep breath, ask the pretty
Waitress for another *cortadito,* and try
My best to smile.

Leaves Falling on the Roof

Leaves falling on the roof, swish
Of wind late at night against the branches,
A sound almost like water moving against
Gravel. Once again, I'm up later than I should be,
My bed empty and uninviting. I scroll
Down a computer screen, listening
To the clock and the air conditioning
In counterpoint, the occasional
Click of the keyboard under my fingers, and
The dog breathing in the corner.
In front of me, tailored men in
Tailored suits give news conferences,
Trying to appear in charge. Others
Pretend to believe them and nod
Accordingly—down the page, the usual
Shots of casualties and collapsing
Cinderblocks. The large events of
The world are far away tonight, but
Regardless hover offshore, tropical
Storm systems that usually
Track north before they reach us.
From satellites, they appear as thick
Clouds moving in obscure, abstract
Patterns, the way God might view
A war, the sobbing and the wounds
Too small to notice.

East of Shark Valley

East of Shark Valley, on the blacktopped
Road to the prison, a hawk lifts himself into
The air and hangs above the high grasses, waiting
For me to pass. From his perspective,
The curls of razor wire along the fence are
Just something shiny reflecting the morning sun. It's
Winter in the Everglades, and the water level is
Down. He will hunt all day, rising with the air currents
And dropping to catch mice, smaller birds, and snakes.
Inside, the prisoners line up for packages, their dull
Blue uniforms an ironic comment on the broad
December sky. Two of my students tell me
About an owl that has taken to perching on the South
Fence at night. "The size of the thing!" one says.
"I was sitting by the window, and I saw these
Wings (he stretches his arms out wide) just shoot up in
Front of me." They debate what kind of owl he is.
No one is sure, but their minds are elsewhere. In
A few days, there's going to be a big transfer. Some of
Them already know they'll be going. They just haven't
Been told where—maybe Homestead or the
Panhandle, a new prison to get used to, new guards
To figure out. The clothes will be the same, though,
Prison blue, and the same thin blankets, and the same
Grits and margarine, maybe the same sausage that feels
Dry and hard in your mouth. Somewhere on the other
Side of the fence, the owl is sleeping, waiting for the
Sun to sink and pinpoint stars to rise.

The Blue Station Wagon

When I woke up in the morning, the windows
Were frosted over from my breath. I'd driven
To New Hampshire the night before, parked the car
By the side of the road, and crawled into a sleeping
Bag in back. It was cold, and I could see the
Beginning of shadows, long bands of light from
The east. I made tea with powdered milk on a brass
Camping stove and watched the sun rise over
Mount Lafayette, the sleeping bag wrapped around
My shoulders. I guess I went hiking that day. I don't
Know where. Was I living in New York then? Cambridge?
To be honest, the place didn't make much difference.
The car where I'd slept was a blue Datsun station wagon
With a fold-down back seat. I'd bought it imagining
Myself traveling across country, along with my wife
And our dog, sleeping on an air mattress, heads poking
Out the tailgate, finding the constellations on a star map.
But, it didn't happen that way. We always stayed in
Motels and hurried back east because Los Angeles wasn't
Any better. When we moved to West 85th Street, between
Columbus and Amsterdam, a junkie smashed in
The passenger-side window one night to steal some
Old clothes and a magnetic chess set. He missed a
Paperback edition of *The Mayor of Casterbridge*, maybe
The Duino Elegies, and some change on the floor. I
Don't think insurance covered the glass.

Looking Backwards

In the picture I wish I'd taken
Twenty years ago, we look like birds

With beards and teeth, our graduation
Robes and hoods flapping black against the

Sky. Our hair is still ungrizzled, our
Eyes excited. It's the last time most

Of us will ever see each other.
In the picture I wish I'd taken

Twenty years ago, we look like ghosts
Of selves we haven't yet become. May

Sunlight makes us sweat beneath our robes.
Do ghosts sweat? A foreign head of state

Gave a speech and received a degree,
Perhaps not in that order. I don't

Remember any of it, only
The sun, our beards, and teeth, maybe a

Handshake and a scroll that wasn't real.
The degree came later through the mail.

In the picture I wish I'd taken
Twenty years ago, I'm not smiling.

Between

In Chicago up near Wrigley Field,
My first grandchild is in utero,
Apparently uninterested
In making a timely appearance.
Here, in Miami, my friend who is
Ninety-one years old dies slowly and
Without knowing anymore who is there
And who is not. He hasn't eaten
Or drunk water for three days. His eyes
Are clouded with a gray film, and he
Doesn't try to move his arms or legs.
I don't know how to make sense of
These comings and goings in the world.
On this side, puddles of rainwater,
Conversations, casualness of
Touch, the taste of hot coffee mixed with
Whiskey, a green landscape, fields planted
With tomatoes or strawberries, sun
In the afternoon, or the time I
Saw dolphins jumping in Biscayne Bay.
On the other, the body aware
Only of itself, reclaiming each
Of the senses, turning them inside
Toward pain and uncomfortable sleep.
There is no balance between the ones
Dying and the ones being born, just
A dim, precarious middle, where
We slide one way or another. On
The radio, Dexter Gordon plays
"Willow Weep for Me." I just listen.

The Life of Things

Armchairs are fetishes of memory, cushions
Sunk into a landscape's fabric, hills, valleys,

The reading lamp casting generous shadows
Across the carpet. Here, my grandfather read me

The first act of *Peer Gynt*—it was years before I learned
There was a second—and the story of Hamlet, more

Told, I think, than read, the velvet upholstery soft
Against my hands as the Prince of Denmark stabbed

Uncle Claudius. The glass doors of the cabinets
Allowed a glance at treasures, vases and ivories, the

Copy of Firdusi's *Epic of Kings* with the etchings
By Alma Tadema, and upstairs my grandmother's portrait

And the drawers filled with stiff white shirts wrapped
In paper. The staircase, wrought iron and wood, swung

In a wide spiral towards sleep or, better, the closet with
The bare light bulb, the stool, a book. Is the memory

Of things just a substitute for hands that knew them,
For the houses we've sold and the vases that smashed

Against the floor? I am older now than my parents were
Then, in that red brick house fronted by live oaks,

Thick pines, and pecans. I've kept the Firdusi, the portrait,
The vases that survived, but none of them shine now

The way they did then. None of them shine.

This and That

At first, memory's uncertain, shaped
By old stories: the Albuquerque
Trip by plane when I was a toddler,
Noise of propellers and shaking, my
Great aunt dying in a dark green room,
The intense sunlight in her kitchen,
A piece of bacon dropped to the floor.
Later, there is clarity of sorts:
My oldest son born just before dawn
In New York, a window that looked out
Over the Hudson, the morning sun
Reflected on the water, and me
Reciting Blake and Donne to try to
Quiet his crying. It didn't work.
Finally, a nurse turned off the lights.
He stopped. *Auden is right. Poetry
Makes nothing happen.* In that marriage,
Memory failed me constantly. We'd
Fight loud enough for all the neighbors
To hear, but next morning, I couldn't
Tell you what it was about, what she'd
Said and I'd said back. Breakfast was
A relief, but we'd stare down into
Our coffee, only the newspaper
For conversation. Cruelty like
Dull scissors cuts unevenly through love,
Leaving threads we pull at years later.

Black Lake

What was new before is now ridiculously antique.
I remember my grandfather's '58 aqua-green Buick:
Fins, red taillights, white roof, and lots of chrome. It
Was an attention-grabber driving down two-lane
Louisiana roads on the way to Black Lake to go
Fishing. We were the modern world rolling by
Unpainted towns, small grocery stores, gas pumps
And silent locals. The fishing guides were silent too,
Seeing no need to say anything. The fish didn't
Like chatter, so we were quiet and sat still
On the narrow bench in the boat, staring at the bright
Lures in the tackle box, threading earthworms
Onto hooks. Mostly, we used bamboo poles and
Patience. The smell of gasoline and fish scales
Mixed with ham sandwiches on white bread and
Deviled eggs. My grandfather fished often and tipped
Well, so the guides liked him. He didn't try to make
Conversation or ingratiate himself, and he didn't
Complain about the heat, the sun's reflection on the
Still, dark water, the mosquitoes. I tried to do
The same, and we stayed out longer than we should.
I came down with heatstroke and was rushed
Home to lie in bed, my mother angry with
My grandfather—one of the only times I remember.
I wasn't allowed to go with him again for at least
A year or two and had to content myself with stories
About one of the guides who got into a knife fight
Or somebody my cousin knew who couldn't understand
Why they wouldn't talk to him and kept pointlessly
Raising his voice. Later, I figured out how to wrap
Ice in a handkerchief and put it under my hat to
Stay cool. My grandfather had died, though, by then.
I inherited the tackle box, the lures, and the casting
Rods I never used well. The Buick went elsewhere.

Scrapbooks

I open the blue Rubbermaid storage box and
Cough from the dust and a chest cold I'm still
Getting over. It's full of old photographs and crumbling

Scrapbooks, notes in my great-aunt's handwriting,
Inventories of jewelry and newspaper articles that mentioned
The family. I remember the chair where my grandfather

Is sitting. It had a green silk cover and was probably
Sold after my father died. My mother is four or five
Years old in the brown-tinted photo, jumping into

Her father's arms. They're both smiling and both
Beautifully innocent. A few years later, he would lose the
House in the Depression, to unexpected margin calls

And, according to family legend, a stock broker
Who really did jump from his Wall Street window.
In another photograph, this one a snapshot made

With a blurry lens, my grandfather is petting my collie
And talking to my mother, a grown woman.
In a year or so, he'll be dead of strokes. I'll wake up

At midnight to hear her scream to my father to call
The rabbi. He survived that one, but wandered around the house
Afterwards in his underwear, confused and tired.

He'll fall onto the Persian carpet in the living room, and
I'll fetch the oxygen tank and feel older than I am.
I stare for a while at their faces. On that Euclidean plane

Of paper and silver oxide, the distance between lives
Can always be divided into an infinite number of points.
The arrow let loose will never reach its target. My mother's features

Will not change either. She will not give birth to me or eventually
Forget my name and my voice. In the brown-tinted photograph,
She'll remain a child, caught in her father's arms, smiling.

Smoke

When my father smoked White Owls or Roi-Tans
In the car with the windows rolled up, I'd
Vomit as though God had pressed a button

On my stomach. Now, he's a photograph,
And my mother a memory from a
Nursing home, her fingers too knotted and

Frozen to pull at the blanket. She was
The size of a child and had lost her teeth—
Only twelve years older than I am now.

A Demitasse

In my sleep my father is neither buried nor in cardiac arrest.
He stands in an old wool jacket, waiting to talk to me.

I don't ask him how long he's been waiting or what he's
Been doing all this time—or why now he wants to see me.

I just shake hands with him, ever formal, and ask if he wants
A cup of coffee. He says "a demitasse" and stares at me

As though there is something he wants to say and can't.
Next, we are sitting on stools in a diner; he leans toward me

And whispers, "I don't blame you anymore for what you told
The doctors"—he means the time his doctors turned to me

For help because he wouldn't listen, kept repeating he was fine.
I had to choose the chemo, and I chose to keep him comfortable, me.

When the cancer came back later, he said it was my fault
That he was dying. The choice I made wasn't up to me.

Then, we are looking at the street. It's somewhere in France, I think.
He got his demitasse and a plate of cookies. He offers me

One, and together we sit on a cast-iron bench and watch people
Pass on bicycles, without talking, my father and me.

Take Solace Where You Can Find It

In 1971, my typewriter was stolen in Jacksonville.
I know just how it happened. I was playing pinball not
Far from the ticket counter, waiting for a bus to New Orleans.
Some kids were chasing each other around the room. One
Brushed past my leg. Two quarters later, I figured things out
And went looking for it: an Olivetti portable in a green case.
Not much luck there, and no alternative but to walk
Through the neighborhood, feeling stupid. I arrived in
New Orleans somewhere around seven in the morning,
And I did some walking there as well. They were washing
The sidewalks, and the stale-sour odors of empty strip clubs
Drained out onto the streets. It was Sunday, and I rested on a park
Bench, watching lines of families spill through the doors of
The Cathedral after Mass. Then I went to The Court of Two Sisters
And had eggs and sausage and coffee and finished it with a brandy.
It didn't bring back the typewriter or the poems that had been
Stored in the case, but I sure as hell felt better.

Apartment on First

The apartment on First was above
A Greek diner called the "Green
Kitchen," but there weren't trees or any
Other greenery nearby, just dull
Gray pavement and yellow taxis that
Parked along the curb. It was summer,
And hot in a way reminiscent
Of Hitchcock's film *Rear Window*, except
Our apartment's only window looked
Out on a narrow airshaft, and our
Neighbors, unlike in the movies, were
Not murderers—or if they were, we
Never noticed. I went to bookstores,
Bought Dorothy Sayers mysteries
And her bad translations of Dante.
We ate Szechuan takeout and pizza.
It all mixes together for me:
Your uncomfortable beanbag chair,
The old Hungarian couple who
Cooked apricot palacsinta in
A restaurant on Third. We'd go there
For lunch and have them with cherry soup
And sour cream. You were so certain
Of what you wanted, your career planned
Meticulously, while I just tried
To balance uncertainty like that
Long stick tightrope walkers carry as
They step ahead, without looking down.
It seemed easier to get married.

The Rockaways

My first wife's grandfather called me a *luftmensch*, a man who
Lives in the air, impractical, flying from one thing to another.

I never disagreed. His own father had been a jailed revolutionary
In Rumania, so he had a reason to value guys with steady jobs.

He and his wife lived in an aging high-rise on Rockaway Beach. It
Smelled of infirmity and furniture covered in plastic. There was

Nothing nearby but other high-rises built to the same model.
They were on the approach route to JFK and shook when jets

Passed overhead. These days, I'm not sure how many places I've
Lived, how many times I've been a student, how many new jobs.

I envy my own grandfather, an attorney most of his life, and
My father, who worked hard and anxiously as a stock broker. I'm

Not like that. I'm afraid there won't be a lot for my children to
Inherit. I've spent too much time with my head in books, days

When I walked around Manhattan photographing shop windows,
Ice machines, random strangers buying hot dogs, or writing poems that

Never worked out, traveling for no good reason. I remember
We spent a month or so housesitting in that high-rise on the beach,

Occupying a life that belonged to someone else. Each day, I'd put on
A jacket and walk the dog down by the ocean, the water only a

Darker shade of gray than the sky, the boardwalk rough and splintered.
By the elevators, there was a machine that sold milk in cartons.

Memorial Drive

There were nights I walked by the Charles River
Dressed in a green army-surplus raincoat and layers of sweaters.
I'd walk all the way down to the bridge by the old Coca-Cola

Bottling Plant and watch the ducks, almost invisible,
Dark feathers floating on even darker water. Walking there,
I thought I could be anywhere, by the Seine in Paris, the Thames

In London—the Liffey was a possibility as well. I had
Followed it once, meandering through Dublin, expecting
Some kind of Joycean experience that never happened. Those

Nights by the Charles were over forty years ago. I only
Remember it was cold, a Cambridge winter, but ice
Hadn't formed yet on the water. The sky and the river

Were sewn from the same black cloth and decorated
With the red Coke sign and lights of passing cars. I suppose
I was lonely in the way only people that age can be

Lonely—always filled with the sense that your life
Will change at any moment. But then it doesn't.
Even if you meet a woman with hair as dark as dark water

Or sky and marry early, you still find yourself going for walks
By the river in the cold, watching black ducks on black
Water, feeling your life could change at any moment.

Road Trip

Days of driving across country, a coyote
Glimpsed running across the highway, a truck stop
In Pecos, Texas late at night, ominous customers
And undrinkable coffee—when I was younger
All this felt exciting: real deserts, real mountains,
Gasoline fumes blown away by the wind. Everything
Real except me. Whoever I was, I hadn't been, and
Whoever I would be, I wasn't yet. In Albuquerque,
The dog ran out in the street and was hit by a car.
He survived, but I had to carry him downstairs at the motel
For days. I fed him hamburgers from MacDonald's
And begged him to live. He did, but was always
A little crazy after that, jumping through closed windows
To chase squirrels, occasionally biting my friends.
I never did the camping I set out to do that year. Instead,
I worked for a few months in LA, developing pictures
In a graphics lab, smelling of chemicals, and never
Seeing daylight. The house where I stayed had no
Air conditioning, so I spent evenings driving the
Freeways, just to stay cool. There were small earthquakes,
But I slept through them. Finally, I drove back east,
Without having gone to the beach or having seen the
La Brea tar pits. I did train the dog not to run out in the street,
But he was never what you'd call obedient. And, whoever
I was then is hard to remember now. The man who drove
Back through the fog and pine trees in Wyoming shares
My name and fingerprints, but not much else. I got
On with my life: work, school, kids, the end of two
Marriages, hundreds of thousands of miles driven,
But none of that happened to him. He stayed somewhere
Between Des Moines and Chicago, left behind
At a gas station.

Reading the Greeks

Each one assigned ten lines, we'd plod through
Things that couldn't be said in English. Outside,
The traffic on Fifth blared as evening settled
Over Manhattan like some luxurious fabric worn
By Mycenean kings or the one Agamemnon
Walked on when he was stabbed. New York seems
So innocent in retrospect, pre-AIDS, pre-9/11, the
Subways loud enough to damage hearing. Up
The street, a sign on the Lone Star Café proclaimed:
"Too Much Ain't Nearly Enough!" What would
Thucydides have made of that? Whatever he
Thought, he'd have written it in strings of Attic
Greek you could use to tie knots. And Socrates?
He'd have said something ironic, while he sat
Naked in the gymnasium across from Alcibiades,
A nameless slave scraping oil from his back
With a stone. In front of me, Amy C., her poems
Already praised by critics, quietly translated extra
Lines. And by the window, Julie H., who wrote for
The New Yorker, knew more than any of us. We were
Regulars, coming back each summer, staring
Into our Liddell-Scotts and verb books while the
Smart money went on vacation. Amy died of cancer,
And Julie's kidneys gave out at 42. And me, whatever
I knew is forgotten, vocabulary, grammar—I only
Remember the stories and how different the Greeks were,
How thought and feelings came from the liver, how quiet
Their world was, the cacophony of automobile engines and
Air conditioning unknown to them, how they watered
Down their wine so they could drink all night and talk,
How Sophocles proved he wasn't senile by reciting
Oedipus at Colonus. Afterwards, I'd go out to Chinatown
And eat soup and dumplings at restaurants I've also
Forgotten—covering my ears in the subway.

Near Columbia

In 1980, I lived in New York City.
My oldest son had yet to be conceived.
There was a Chinese restaurant on Broadway
That served noodles in soup for lunch to Asian
Students, and the bookstore next door carried all
The literary journals. That block across
From the campus seems like heaven to me now,
With everything you'd need for life on Earth:
A refugee chocolatier, her recipes from
Vienna or Budapest, I forget which,
And a coffee house where you could sit all day.
For jazz, there was a station in New Jersey.
When Borges came to speak that year, I lined
Up early to find a seat down front. He wore
A deep blue suit and leaned on a carved walking
Stick. I don't remember much he said,
Only that he was patient with the crowd.
Milosz read across town a few months later,
And I wandered in a daze to the crosstown bus.
Here, in the center of the universe, I ate
Cinnamon *babka* and tried to write poems.

A Steady Stream

There's a leak in the roof I don't have money to fix.
That's because when you fix one thing, there's always
Two others that need fixing, that have to be done now
Before the rain starts, a steady stream of things—not
Just the drip of a leak only noticed when you glance
At darkened plaster and see the shape of Argentina
On the ceiling. If you touched it, the Andes
Would crumble into the sink. The coils
Of the air conditioning are just as bad—rusted
Through, the man said. They too could crumble.
The carpets have stains of someone else's life.
What did they spill in the bedroom? And from a bacchanalia,
Which the dictionary tells me is drunken revelry? Or was it
Diet Coke spilled while watching television, when someone
Scored a goal? Does this stain commemorate a victory,
Or just an accident? And then, there's the glass door
With a crack concealed by clear tape. I imagine a crime scene—
The tape a different color. If I looked hard enough,
There'd be other things to fix as well. A responsible man
Would begin somewhere, but that's not me. Each repair
Opens a door to others, a process that while not infinite
Is still consuming. "What did you do with your life, Mr. Franklin?"
Don't worry, I fixed everything.

Rain

Rain on the roof doesn't let up, the noise
Not romantic or soothing. It's the sound
Of anxious nerves sending messages, neurons
Leaping synapses, Morse code of migraines.
We spoke on the phone a short time ago.
You were worried, your work, family. I
Wasn't much different. After a while, the
Conversation drifted to poetry, the way it
Always does with us: Li Qingzhao, Yosano
Akiko, Landor's poem to his son, Carlino.
After a while, we both felt better, even though
The day hadn't gone as planned, the poems we'd
Hoped for hadn't arrived, and the time wasted
Would not return. For all that, we felt better.
I wish you were here now to lie down next to me,
To curl together beneath the sheets, the soft blanket,
The roof pounded by rain. I'd like to smell
Your thick hair and feel your lips on my shoulder.
The thunder has moved farther away. The rain
Is slower now and falters. The poems we talked
About, full of desire, regret, smooth bodies, and
Hands suddenly old, poems carved out of jade
And wanting—how strange that they comfort us.
Tomorrow, we'll probably worry about that as well,
But for now, we'll both fall asleep, you in your
Apartment, me here listening to the last drops
Splatter on the roof, smelling your hair fresh
From the shower.

II. Without Footprints

Caravaggio at the Execution of Beatrice Cenci

The others' sentences were worse, the head of
Her brother, for example, smashed open with a mallet—
The story of the murder an act of vengeance, love
Or greed, depending on who might tell it.

The painter probably didn't care which.
He was there to sketch what otherwise
Happens too quickly to observe. "Bitch!"
One woman yelled, and Beatrice's eyes

Glanced in her direction as barefoot
She walked across the scaffold to the block.
She could not look at the executioner who put
Her neck in place. Somewhere, a clock

Sounded, iron on iron, and a friar prayed
Loudly to be heard above the crowd, the chime
Of noontime bells. The short blade
Rose not slowly or too fast. There was time

To draw his arm weighted in mid-air.
Then, the axe dropped hard across the curve of spine and skin,
And arteries streamed blood onto the face and hair
Hanging by a muscle in her neck. The executioner swung again.

Cinders

We aspired to better things, my sisters and I,
Sacrificed so much. We cut off toes
So our feet would pass the test. Blood
Smeared on the glass of the slipper.
All the time, though, she was watching,
Bringing rags and water to clean the knife. Her humility
Was a disguise. She was expert at biding her time,
Blushing modestly as she danced with the prince,
Using witchcraft—call it what it is.
She hid the white delicacy of her hands
Under soot from the chimney fire. She claimed
She had no comb to make her hair presentable.
Lies, all of it. The Devil knows what she put
In our food when she'd hover over the pot.
He also knows what secrets he whispered, while
She stared greedily at the bubbling of the
Stew, dancing lumps of meat, turnips,
Whatever else was there. We were not rich.
Our food was simple. She smiled and
Pretended she wasn't hungry.
We were idiots not to recognize her duplicity.
It was only when the birds pecked out
Our eyes that we could see her.

Goya

Because of all he saw, seeing it all
Was unbearable. He moved to The House
Of the Deaf Man, already deaf himself.
In a black mood, he painted on the walls,
In oil, the Black Paintings. If he could paint
Subjects more grotesque than what he had seen,
Then what he had seen might seem less grotesque.
He lived surrounded by monstrosity:
Saturn devouring his son, crucifix-
Like torso and legs, decapitated
By the huge black mouth, torn by the bloody
Grip of his hands, startled eyes, black nostrils.
If he could paint away madness, madness
Might vanish. Mock the inquisitors, and
They might vanish too. Turn them to witches
Surrounding the great he-goat of evil,
And they might rise up in the air, weightless.
Before he slept, he thought of Pepita
Naked, clothed, her wicked smile taunting him—
Before he lived surrounded by monsters.

Schopenhauer

Schopenhauer spoke of suicide
During the dessert course, the spoon for
The trifle unlikely to do much
Damage and the cheese knife too dull to
Penetrate his woolen vest. No one
Thought to ask for his shoelaces or
The belt his stomach exceeded. He
Was a great man, and great men often
Say silly things, sometimes translated
From Greek or Sanskrit: Never to have
Been born is best. All things are on fire.
But later, after everyone had
Gone to bed, he sat alone close to
The fireplace, a brahman reciting
Vedas before the sacrificial
Flame. What god heard him as thought dissolved,
As he stared at this marriage of wood
And burning heat, the glow of dying
Things, a log that could have been a corpse?

Respect

We sat in a circle, and one student read a rhyming poem about being beaten by his father until the blood pooled on the floor.

The other students nodded. A few said the same thing had happened to them.

Beyond the windows and the fence, the sun refused to blink. Relentless afternoon heat turned the earth hard and brittle. White cranes cowered in the tall grass.

The father's anger never makes sense. His belt cuts the air before it cuts skin. No one ever stops him, and he'll die without ever talking about it.

If there is a scream, it's lost in the air, rising soft and slow as a cloud—puffy, shapeless, pushed west by the wind. If there is a scream, it hides itself like a crane in the tall grass, small claws clasping dust and roots. No matter how closely you listen, you won't hear it.

The boy says nothing, and for forty years the scream lives in his stomach, a parasite that eats from every spoonful of his food, that grows, a shapeless gray cloud in his guts.

He reads the poem, but it doesn't change anything. The parasite is still there, making him bleed from the inside out, hiding in the tall grass of his breathing, even at night when he sleeps. The other men in the class know all about this. Each of them looks at his own stomach, shifts in the chair. They start to tell stories about hunting, about killing deer with twelve-gauge shotguns loaded with slugs, how there's a white spot on the neck that you aim for, how some places you can't hunt with a thirty-ought-six because the bullet travels too far.

One of them asks me what I'm going to do today, after class. I say, "work," which is a lie, because I don't want to talk about how I'll get in the car and go shopping, about all the choices I have for spending this afternoon, how wherever I go, there'll be air conditioning, cold beer, things to buy, how I'll eat dinner with my son and watch a movie.

Afterwards, I walk toward the gate and the sharp spiral of wire above the fence. Every few minutes, there are loud volleys of shots, guards practicing in groups on a firing range, out of sight, practicing for the day when they'll hold their pistols in front of them with both hands, aim, and fire at men who are not made of paper. They pause just long enough to reload.

When It's Difficult

All day it's threatened to rain—a smell in the air, slightly metallic, exhaust rising hot when I roll down the car window, clouds hanging low over the ocean. From the highway, lines of gray water falling off to the west.

In one of my cases, a child turns anxious, makes accusations to a teacher. In the courtroom, we ask the same questions but receive different answers. Later, I sit in Dunkin Donuts and drink weak coffee, think about how hard it is to live in uncertainty.

This is one of those afternoons I want to walk through Home Depot and smell lumber, the corpses of pine trees, of hardwood too. The saws only lack a magician and his beautiful assistant. The wood only lacks bark and roots, long limbs and green leaves. Perhaps I will find you by the light fixtures or plumbing supplies. Perhaps you are watching me from behind the batteries.

In the middle of summer, the evening arrives slowly and with some measure of deliberation. If I wanted to see the sun set, I would have to find a tall building or a bridge. So instead, I sit with the lights off, watching shadows reach in through the windows.

Access Denied

I won't be going to teach today. The prison
Found an excuse to shut us down, another way
To regulate, to punish. I'm not surprised, but I hadn't
Expected it, if that makes any sense. So, now,
I won't be making the drive south, between
Palm tree farms and tract housing, homes built
So close to the Everglades alligators crawl
Into the backyards at night to hunt small dogs
And cats. The Mexican restaurants are pretty
Good down there, though—families eating
Tortillas and laughing, a toddler with salsa
Dripping from her chin, and sometimes men
Sitting alone, everyone they care about thousands
Of miles away. My students weren't all that different.
Some of their families had given up on them,
Some said they might forgive them eventually. One
Or two would say their husbands, parents, were
Waiting for them. But, families don't really enter
This place. Even if there are visits, they don't know
What it's like. Wives, daughters, are hard to
Recognize dressed in sagging blue cotton and
Black work boots, the way they listen for the
Guard's quick orders, or how their eyes circle
The room. Visitors don't understand lines
Marked on a walkway, or a C.O. writing you
Up because one day you just lost it and talked
Back. The Department says it's changing
Lives, one at a time. For some reason, I find
That scarier than whatever dishonesty, drugs, or
Violence brought them here in the first place. In prison,
You've got meds or God or both, but you don't have
Anything like the life you had before you got here.
I can't imagine what those changed lives will look like.
Whatever I was doing teaching classes, I wasn't
Trying to change anybody. I'd bring poems
Or copies of a book, and we'd talk. They'd bring
What they'd written and read it out loud, some
Mumbling, others performing. I just know they

Had a good time for a little while before they went
Back to their dorms to be counted. That may be
Over now, the program cancelled—none of us
Allowed back in. I keep thinking they'll wonder
Where we are today, why we're not there, why there's
No call-out for classes. Rumors will fill in the gaps.
They'll say it had something to do with the yoga
Teacher who was caught with drugs, or that one of us
Tried to bring in a cellphone. Ultimately, it won't
Matter. In his office, the assistant warden, back from
Lunch, will sit behind his state-purchased desk and spend
The afternoon reading spreadsheets.

In the Waiting Room

The waiting room was a cliché: copies of
The New Yorker and *The New York Review of Books*,
Metal chairs, walls painted white, neutrally decorated.

*

What I don't think I ever said was how afraid I was,
How much I wanted to desire, to be desired,
But how hard that is sometimes. Last night I held you
As though we were up in a high place and
You could keep me from falling, as though I could slip
Inside your skin, become your heartbeat or
Your breath. I used to imagine the self as a paramecium,
A small squirming organism dressed up in
Clothes and ideas. When we're together,
The clothes and ideas vanish, all that abandoned,
Nothing left except feeling. It takes so much to hold
Each other this way, skin pressed against skin,
Knowing there is nothing left of me, of you.

*

My analyst lived in an old Victorian house
In Massachusetts. I never knew much about her.
There's a journalist on the radio, though,
Whose voice is similar to hers, a Mid-Atlantic
Accent that I grew used to, while I was faced away,
Reclining, talking without restraint. Mostly, she would ask
Questions, and I would answer, ramble on,
Hoping I'd say something unintended,
The glimpse in the mirror.

*

This was the time when my first marriage
Was ending, my wife angry, impatient. I
Avoided her. Close to bedtime, I would go
Shopping at Star Market—the one that looked out

Over the turnpike—walking up and down
Cold, empty aisles, standing by my cart
reading magazines, wondering if
I'd been out long enough for her to fall asleep.

*

*I'm back in that Victorian house, in
The waiting room, reading one of Frederick Crews'
Attacks on Freud when the door to the stairway opens.
Wives, lovers, friends, even family members I haven't
Seen since I was a child—they all crowd in, looking
For a place to sit down. I'm annoyed, but I
Get up and offer my seat to someone, I don't remember
Who, and give up reading the article. The sun
Pours in through the windows, and the bodies of
These visitors cast shadows across each other.
The air grows thick and uncomfortable. I feel congested
In my sinuses and remember Freud's correspondence
With Wilhelm Fliess, describing his mucus. An
Elderly cousin asks why I'm not in the army like her
Nephew. I explain I'm a teacher, but she doesn't
Pay any attention. My father and mother are sitting
Together in the corner, speaking in low voices. I
Want to tell them something, but I can't think of what.
Another woman, one I loved, is looking for a water
Fountain, but it doesn't exist. She is thirsty and pacing.
Then a bird flies into the window, breaking
The glass. It lies dead on the floor, but
Outside the hole left by that small body, there's a vacuum
Sucking everyone out, one by one. As they vanish,
They seem to elongate, a thinning effect. I hear
My analyst's voice telling me to come in because it's
5:00. The bird is still dead on the floor. Its
Feathers glisten.*

A Guest

It's not late at night, but it feels like it is.
For a few days now, I've heard
Something moving behind me, present
As I pick up the phone or type a letter,
Wash dishes or a load of clothes. It doesn't
Announce itself out loud, but I can hear it
Breathing, waiting for me to notice, to
Speak. If loneliness had a body, it would
Sit at the table and eat. It would tell stories,
Recall the time when an antique chair
Collapsed beneath a friend, or when I got drunk
In Ireland on my honeymoon. The stories
Would not always be funny. That one
Ends predictably, with vomiting in the bathroom.
Loneliness would remember things like
That, and tonight, I would not stand in the kitchen,
Listening, staring at the bananas and the salt.
The presence of all that is not here would
Keep me company.

Sadness

I talk about sadness as though she were a dinner guest
Who's overstayed her welcome. It's one in the morning and
She's still here chattering about philosophy, asking for more wine.

I talk about sadness as though she were cleaning windshields
At a stoplight, pleading for quarters or, better still, dollar bills.
She is persistent, it's true, and undeterred by switching off the light.

But, I know I've got it all wrong about sadness. She waits
On my bookshelf to be taken down and opened. She's patient
And oddly reassuring. She says she'll always be here

After everyone else isn't. She'll go for walks with me
And observe the formation of clouds, how tree limbs are shaped
By the wind. She'll remind me to bring a scarf.

Barcelona

I imagine you on a cold day in Barcelona, wind
Lashing the spires of Sagrada Família and the palm trees
By the beach dreaming of Africa, listening
To obscenities shouted by the waves.
I imagine you with a leather coat
And lapis earrings and a blouse almost
As smooth as your skin. There is a glass
Of wine in front of you and inside the wine
A little fire. We finished talking a long time ago,
But neither one of us has the courage to leave.

Ghazal

You can make a poem out of air, she said.
I disagreed. Poems require dirt and spit, I said.

It was a holiday afternoon, and the stores were closed.
All the buses were on night schedule, the paper said.

There was a café open with plastic chairs, a radio playing euro-pop.
Footballers were waiting to get their palms read, the waitress said.

It was a holiday afternoon when it began to rain.
Poems dripped from the ceiling into buckets that said

"In case of the fire"—splattering in time to the music.
They fall from either handkerchiefs or anthologies, she said.

I disagreed: "Go look in the buckets, and you'll see."
They want to know their future, the waitress said.

Anywhere

It could be anywhere in Europe—cobblestones, chimneys, clothes hanging from a line in front of the windows.

A car, some variation on a Fiat, is parked half-on, half-off the sidewalk.

There is a café on the corner, nothing chic, outside plastic tables and chairs, a waitress is checking her cell phone. She frowns and then straightens some cups. Inside, they set out sandwiches behind glass.

If you were dreaming this place, the waitress, the car, the sandwiches, you would know where you were. You would sense this was an industrial town in the Veneto or Croatia. You would know it's almost lunch time.

Instead, you look at your feet, at the dust on your shoes, and wonder how long you've been walking. Behind you, a neighborhood ends at the gates of a factory. The streets curve away into other streets and lives you won't understand.

You might have come here with a woman once. This might be a memory that has stuck with you. Only, it isn't. You've never been here before, but you've been to a hundred places just like it.

The sun is covered briefly by a cloud, and men walk out from the factory down the street. Voices move past you, talking rapidly in one of the all-too-many languages you don't speak.

You reach in your pocket to see if you have money. Whose picture is on the bill? Are they Euros? You're getting hungry and wonder if you have enough to buy something. Maybe a coffee and some kind of pastry.

It's only then you remember your passport, tucked away inside your jacket. You reach for it, but the ink of your name has smeared. Your picture is no longer visible.

Poem of the Street

Waned two nights from full, the moon steers west
Above my head, over the ranch-style houses of the street.

There was a time we held each other. Everything
Was already over, but we held each other on this street.

Sound carries at night. From far away an engine whines—
Over the speed limit, but never leaving the street.

What can I salvage from our life? Biology made me a creature
With lungs and feet. The white moon throbs over the street.

Moving

I'd lived there long enough to be sad
At leaving. The mangoes I planted
Were bearing heavy fruit. The devil
Tree towered over the house, its thorns
The size of my fist, its pink blossoms
Carpeting the bricks. Hibiscus blooms,
Deep red, startled the eye. I'd gotten
Used to my footsteps on hallway tile.
I knew the cabinets and the drawers.
Even my disorderly bookshelves
Were at home there. (Writers were not
Placed next to the colleagues they despised.)
The new place would be smaller, with less
Room for echoes, missing furniture
And other voices besides my own.
I'd still have a desk, stacks of papers,
Photographs. After a while the rooms
Would even smell the same: incense, old
Books, cleaning fluid, onions frying
In the kitchen, the dog when he comes
In from the rain, laundry freshly washed.
It would be the same but not the same.
Months earlier, I planted a tree,
An ylang-ylang, by the walkway.
I knew then I was leaving, so I
Don't know why I bothered. Still, it did
Please me to imagine the scented
Yellow blossoms hanging in front of
That ranch-style house on that random street.

Over Coffee

It's my third cup of coffee, on Saturday.
It's not that I'm tired, not on Saturday.

In the cup, hot milk swirls till dark,
The way we used to walk at twilight on Saturday.

I drink coffee and sit remembering the tight
Weave of your fingers with mine on Saturday.

Sometimes it's hard to separate desire from affection,
And hard to know which you want on Saturday.

I admit it, I'm a bad Jew. I don't pine for Jerusalem, recite
The blessings, or walk to shul in a white shirt on Saturday.

I have my own way of celebrating the Sabbath now: over coffee
In the shade, remembering your face full of desire on Saturday.

A Friend Asks How I Write a Poem

Trying to write a poem is like
Trying to have an erection. I'm
Not saying it doesn't work for some
Guys, just not for me. So, first I sort
Of wish for it, then I give up and
Make a cup of coffee. My poems
Are full of coffee as a result.
Next, I look at the spines of books on
The shelf, read names like Borges, Blake, and
Christina Rossetti. It's a lot
Like praying, which also doesn't work.
The last resort is walking around
The backyard with the dog jumping all
Over trying to get me to throw
Him one of many toys lost in the
High grass. Finally, I give in. I
Pick up a dirty blue squish-ball that
Squeaks when he bites it and heave it all
The way down by the gate. He runs to
Get it like he's been waiting for this
Moment his whole life. He's all fur and
Wind, with the ball in his mouth and a
Slightly insane look in his eyes. I
Can't help laughing. I've forgotten all
About trying to write a poem.

Allegory of Grief

The delivery man knocked loudly on
The door, and I signed for the package,
Wrapped tight in brown paper, tough cardboard,
Tape. It took scissors and persistence.
When I looked up, the sun had
Already dropped below the tree line.
My empty stomach told me it was
Time for dinner. But, I couldn't stop
Looking at this new appliance I'd
Purchased, adjusting the dial, puzzling
Over the instructions, schematics,
Feeling its white enamel cool in
My palms, my fingertips. I thought that
If I stared at it long enough, I'd
Begin to understand how it worked.

A Few Days Later

Every tree the hurricane didn't
Knock down, it cut back, until they all
Offered what landscapers call "light shade."

Their leaves gleaming like bright green coins in
Afternoon sun, they move carefully,
Along with the breeze, not leaning too

Far one way or the other. Having
Survived, now the limbs must get used to
Being alive all over again.

Lives of the Stars

*The moon has set and
the Pleiades also....*
        — Sappho

It's November now. The Pleiades
Return, traveling west each night. In
The books, they sound like they act in porn
Or strip for a living, "middle-aged,
Hot B-type stars," the Seven Sisters.
It's kind of embarrassing really.
They kept company with Greek sailors
Off the shores of Turkey in winter.
The sailors would watch them heading home
Each night, perhaps to some dive in the
Piraeus where they'd rent rooms upstairs,
Or farther west to Italy. Their
Rising marked the season of travel,
Soft lights in the sky, ill-defined but
Visible nonetheless, their G-strings
Hung like pearls on the horn of a bull.

The Cyclops

Regardless of his appetites, Polyphemus the Cyclops
Lived a simple life, herding his sheep, calling every now and then
To his brothers who lived on other mountains with other sheep.
In the winter, his cave was warm, and there was firelight—
And shadows that moved across the walls like perfect thoughts,
Flickering for a moment, then moving on. When he slept,
He slept surrounded by the wool and snorts of ewes and rams,
As they shifted their bodies closer, then farther from the fire.
If he was thirsty, he grabbed the teats of a ewe and squirted
Warm milk into his mouth, swallowing before it overflowed
His lips. He had no books or musical instruments, but he had
The black sky and constellations swaying overhead. He spoke to them,
And occasionally they would answer: the Dioscuri, Orion, the Bull.
When he was hungry, he'd choose the largest ram, roasting it in the fire
Until the fat ran clear, and the flesh smelled of wood smoke.
The rest of the flock looked away at those times, embarrassed at
How easily one of their own could become meat and marrow. He
Would soothe them then, running his thick fingers through
Their curls, telling them not to worry, that he wasn't hungry anymore,
That they, with their sad eyes and pink tongues, were his favorites.
But when the Cyclops looked out across the horizon and saw white
Sails cut through the waves and drop anchor in the bay and distant,
Ant-like figures crossing the brown sand, his stomach felt hollow and
Saliva pooled behind his teeth. Poor Polyphemus, who never could
Distinguish loneliness from hunger!

Without Footprints

I read a book once by a Jungian on the soul.
He used words from the Greek myths and the

New Testament, so I thought of the soul living
On an Aegean beach, sunbathing and walking

On the sand without leaving footprints. Perhaps,
She was perfume made from orange blossoms and

Lavender, and was joined to all the other souls
The way a field of heather sways in the wind.

Metaphors like this take you absolutely nowhere.
You think of yourself as a crystal elaborating

Itself, each jagged edge pointing in a different
Direction. You think you're eternal as the sky

Over green waves when they break on the sand,
Gravel, the crushed shells of mollusks and creatures

Too small for God to care about. It could be
The seashells and the sunsets are reluctant to

Disillusion you, or maybe you just haven't heard
What they whisper. On the sixth day, after creating

Animals and things that crawl, God created man and
Said that naming all this was up to him. We were

So new to the world, you can't blame us for getting
It wrong. We mixed up names with the things we

Pointed at. We turned to the elephant with tusks
Gleaming in sunlight, and said "elephant," imagining

We'd created something too. Then, enthusiastic,
We even named things that weren't there and thought

That made them real. We said "justice," "property,"
"Society," "self." It was late at night before we

Stopped. Then, looking at each other in the silver
Glare of moonlight—fire hadn't been invented yet—

We gave each other names as well, almost drunk
With how special we'd become, how individual.

That's when someone, exhausted by naming,
Mumbled "soul" as his eyes closed and everyone else

Leaned in to listen. "Soul," we repeated, "soul."

Pigeon Wings

The grotesque is not a category of our lives. We
Never imagine ourselves with mouths open, staring

From the stone facade of a cathedral, pigeon
Wings draped like laurel across our skulls.

In the campo, the bearded statue of a novelist,
Unknown to me, watches sternly the adolescents

Sprawled across his steps—cigarettes and
Cell phones dangling loose and eyes looking

Everywhere but at each other. They wear
Their hearts on their t-shirts and, when the

Shadows of palazzi and tourist hotels lean over
Their heads, drift away to cafes and drinks.

I can see light spreading from the *piano nobile*
That looks onto the canal—a reception for

A visiting film director or other luminary. Well-
Dressed women and their uncomfortable men

Walk up the steps. I see you standing by a shop
Window, considering an album of hand-made paper.

I want to take your hand and walk with you
Back through the courtyard of our building, past

Iron gates and doors with unfamiliar keys, fold back
The bedspread and compare memory with the smell

Of your hair, the shape of your hips and
Calves, your thighs that open to me, while

From the window we hear the splash of water,
Footsteps, and voices. None of this will ever

Happen. We are not in Italy, and what was between us
Will not be repeated. Memory is both baroque

And cruel, and I am like that gargoyle,
My mouth locked open, staring.

Montage

Begin with strips of light left over from
Splicing reels of celluloid: an image
Of a woman's hand, a horse bolting,
Bees circling a flower, slanted sunlight,
The horse's hooves, and motes of pollen.
A man and a woman walking somewhere
Isolated—while a trolley car winds
Through Zurich, Einstein
Thinks relativity into being, the woman's
Hand holds on to a railing, the ship
Pulls away, and dinner waits steaming
On the table, but the chairs are empty.
During the blitz, a Polish refugee plays
Mozart in the tube beneath Trafalgar Square.
Walls crumble. Some moments are black and
White and even silent. Others are in colors so
Rich they make our eyes hurt—but on a small
Table gloved fingers flatten and assemble the
Curling strips, rearrange them into one order and
Then another. In this story, the hero survives.
In that one, he dies. The poem can open
And close the same way regardless. Bees
Circle a flower. Autumn sunlight. A woman's hand.

Phone Call

After midnight, and you called, I guess, to wish me a happy new year.
You sounded a little drunk, but that was already last year.

Through the telephone, I could hear your voice
Trying to speak over others—so much can happen in a year.

I still don't know why you called then, or what you wanted so badly
To tell me. I think I heard you say that getting over love sometimes
takes a year.

I had already gone to bed when you called, sinking into sleep
Where a day or a minute is no different from a year.

When I tried to phone the next day, your voicemail
Told me to leave a message, that you would call back next year.

Oddly Shaped Windows

What the eye sees in rain is an oblong lens,
Mobius time looped in a blue-gray strip

Beneath a microscope, aluminum
Skies and oddly shaped windows.

What the eye sees in itself is the cataract's
Soft blur, reflected glare, and doubled sight.

We are moved by imperfection because it
Makes us feel at home, the screen door never

Quite shut, the wood porch settled at the corner.
Hold up a magnifying glass to your hand,

And follow the contours across dry, pink skin.
Broken by creases, rivers, arroyos in the high

Desert, the lines on your palm tell
The past not the future, how you have let go

Of all you ever grasped, how you have held on
To something you couldn't hold.

Behind your eyes, it's always raining. Water
Splatters against the roof shingles and shapes itself

To whatever it embraces—the perfect lover.
What the eye sees in rain is the reflection

Of its own desire, always approaching.
What the eye sees in rain is the gray wind

Moving across the lagoon at sunset, is the ruin
Of a boathouse, the wake of passing ships.

Venice Weather

When I walked outside this morning, it
Was Venice weather, cool, cloudy, the
Street full of puddles from last night's rain.
A wind from the bay carried the smell
Of salt water and the bones of fish.

I'd been perseverating about
A friend's death, the selfishness of grief,
The conversations you have with a
Person incapable of reply—
His imagined response: "Why bother?"

If I were in Venice, espresso
In hand, I'd be thinking the same thoughts,
But looking up the Giudecca
Canal—Palladio's plague-born church,
Extravagant in the face of loss.

A seagull's wet swooping reminds me
Of Isola di San Michele,
Of Brodsky's grave, near Diaghilev's
And, oddly, Pound's, those pens readers left,
So many pens, notes, flowers turning

Brown at the edges of the petals.
At Columbia, I'd studied with
Brodsky, watched him build his pyramids
Of cigarette filters, memorized
Auden, Frost, argued with him even

Though I knew he was probably right.
There was a young Russian woman with
Black hair standing by the grave. She'd come
All that way to thank him, to speak to
Someone who would never hear her voice.

In Venice's afternoon, amber
Sunlight seeped through the clouds, reflecting

Off the red rooftiles, paving stones, and
The wake of vaporettos crossing
The lagoon, but in the parking lot

Of my townhouse next to the golf course,
Two blocks from a shopping mall, the same
Sun gleams on what's left of the rain. I
Stop as I lift my grocery bags.
A flock of white birds pick through the grass.

III. The Way It Is Now

The Way It Is Now

Two nights ago, you asked me if I felt old,
And I had trouble answering. I settled for a joke
And said I just felt immature, but we both knew
I was lying. There are futures I've already passed,
Poorly-marked intersections where, I guess, I
Could have turned left, or right, and didn't. That's
What age is: time made real in your body, the way
Bone rubs away at bone, voice grows rough,
Memory thickens into a meandering line of
Choices, accidents, each one redefined by the
Next. *So much for intentions.* I check the time
On my cellphone and lie in the dark, thinking of
Mountains in New Hampshire, a trail I hiked,
Alone, years ago, stumbling over tree roots,
Slipping in spring mud. I remember a dinner of
Oatmeal and chocolate, the smell of drying socks.
Later, *Sonnets to Orpheus* by flashlight, the call
Of an owl in the maple trees. Barefoot but awake,
I let the dog out back and sit with hot coffee
In the blue, pre-dawn light—the color of
Water covering white sand or the earth
Seen from space. Every time I look up, the sky
Brightens more. There are fewer shadows.

In Your Country

I've never been to your country. I only know it in the smell
Of frying onions, some garlic, of red beans and cornmeal,
In translated novels and the hiss of someone steaming milk for coffee, the exhaust
Of a passing car on a wet street, in a cotton dress hung like a flag in front of a shop.
On the steps of a church, a family poses for wedding pictures with a priest.
Everyone is elegantly dressed and smiles except the priest. (Each year,
There are more civil ceremonies, and abortions. He does not believe their excuses.)
The family crowds into a van and waves to people they don't know. The van
Gets smaller, turns left, and disappears.
In a crowded bookstore, a girl with shoulder-length hair reads poems
Until her cellphone rings. She buys the book, hurries off.
For some reason, I think of sweaters being knitted in a small house,
A group of women chatting, their fingers moving like clever machines,
Their eyes dark and bright at the same time. Outside, it gets cold in
The evening. Leather shoes descend from buses, a cigarette butt
Arcs and falls still glowing in the gutter, laughter, aguardiente, a football game
On television, the screen emerald green, faces and flags I don't recognize.
In the bathtub, soapy water swirls counter-clockwise, the opposite of here. The stars
Are unfamiliar too, but the moon at least is the same.
Perhaps you can see it from your window,
A piece of broken porcelain drifting to the west.

For a While

We sat in the car with the engine
Running. In Florida, you need the

Air conditioning, even at night,
Even near the water. The streetlights

Turned the sidewalk bronze, a strange color,
But we'd parked in the privacy of

Oak trees, limbs pulled over us like a
Blanket, the air thick with our breathing.

Letting Go

It's a quiet morning, a little jet traffic
Overhead, but otherwise only the random
Sounds of neighbors and wind in the oak trees,
The dog shaking himself, moving from one
Side of the house to another. Now would be
A good time to be honest, to think about
How I don't know what love is anymore, what
Desire means, how often my feelings are
Unknown to me. I should start by telling you
That I'm still in my robe. I haven't shaved or
Showered. My hair's uncombed and grayer
Than usual. Making coffee today felt like
An achievement. Last night, we sat in the car
And talked about wanting. It was late, and
I had to get home. But, I felt your breath on my
Cheek, and something let go inside me. I wanted
To feel myself disappear inside you. I
Wanted not to feel myself at all. What I'll
Say next is blasphemy, but I don't apologize.
There are moments with you, in bed or touching
When I'm no longer there, extinguished
Like a candle. No subject, no verb, only that
"Dazzling darkness" Vaughan wrote about and
San Juan de la Cruz—your favorite. They
Knew it as the presence of God. I don't, only
That the mind falters, words stop. Schopenhauer
Knew it too, how we can lose ourselves entirely, become
Something else we don't understand. You'll tell me
This poem has gone on too long, become too
Discursive. Maybe you're right. Maybe I should
Have stuck to remembering your lips and fingers,
The way we held each other, the headlights
Of cars moving down the street in the dark.
But it's too late now for that. I told you I wanted
To be naked with you, to let go of the person I've

Tried to be, of all the protective gestures and
Images, the wounded self that wants another to
Make it whole. All this is why I don't understand
Desire anymore, or love, and why I'm writing to you,
Here in my bathrobe, the coffee cup empty,
Except for a few drops, cold now against my tongue.

Chatter of Rain

Chatter of rain on the roof, summer
Arriving, a guest with suitcases
Settling in for a humid visit.
Nights with mosquitoes, brown moths drawn to
The sliding-glass door, the rumble of
The air conditioner, and books left
Open on the couch, sweat collecting
In odd places on my body, sheets
Too warm, but the fan too cool. I'll reach
To touch you, but you'll have flown off to
Another continent where winter
Makes you pile on blankets and shiver
A little in the dark, beneath a
Different configuration of stars.
Ximena, I miss you already.

You Joke

Calling me a *gringo arrecho*, a horny gringo.
Undoubtedly, you're right. It's shameful to feel

So much, the pull of hands and groins, of lips and teeth,
The way our bed has its own echoes, not sound but

Movement, my sometimes-clumsy hands on fragile
Porcelain, shaking as I balance the small cups and saucers

That rest between your thighs, the salt-metal taste
Of sweat on your neck's white nape, my sudden

Exhalation when your fingers stroke my forearm.
I know there is some part of me that's broken, the

Snapped spring of a pocket watch. I can't keep track
Of the time or believe you desire me this way. I can't

Trust my tongue tracing lines of your lips or my hands
That want, of their own accord, to reach inside you, drawn

To your magnetic heart, your breasts against my cheek.
In bed, we laugh, then gasp, finally fall back

Trembling, curled tight together. One of the candles
I'd lit sputters, goes out, and a blues guitarist I don't

Recognize plays something good on the radio,
Remembers a woman who was better than he was,

One he didn't deserve.

A Certain Age

When you get to a certain age, friends
Start to die. It's hard to believe that
You argued politics together
A week or so ago, now nothing.
You start to understand the old guys
At the deli, who prop up spoons in
White coffee cups, break their cookies in
Half, and declare in New York accents:
There're too many fucking funerals.
Now, it's my friend Frank, dying slowly
Or not, but losing interest in
Staying alive. His books don't leave the
Shelf, he can't sit without support, and
His sheets smell of urine no matter
How often they're changed. He mostly eats
Scrambled eggs and toast. It scares the hell
Out of me—not the cancer or the
Pain, but the slow, unshaven sinking,
The way your appetites drop to the
Floor and your eyes grow dull. Frank must hate
That: how his speech has slowed, how tired his
Tongue gets in mid-sentence, how he wants
To get up but stays in bed, knowing
His legs won't get him even to the
Refrigerator or the bathroom.
There's nothing smart or good I can say
About any of this. The body
Breaks as though bones were thin pieces of
Metal, left out in the rain, rusted,
And the mind isn't any better.
Frank, I'm glad we drank good wine with our
Dinners. I'm glad you liked Ximena's
Lentil soup and my ratatouille.
I'm sorry I can't do more for you.

Origami

She takes a sheet of white paper
And breaks it in a knife-sharp fold.
The edge could draw blood.

She takes an edge, cracking
The ribs of paper. If paper
Could cry out, it would shriek
Like a bird, a crane
Penetrated by a hunter's arrow.

She takes a crane and breaks
Its wing. White is the color
Fear leaves behind when it
Passes through bone.

She takes a bone from a hunter
And folds it till she has a knife.

She takes a sheet stained with blood
And balances it on the edge
Of a bird, a wing.

A Great Emptiness

In Sung landscapes, there is often a
Great emptiness, cloudy and off to
One side, as though the universe could
Dissolve without anyone's notice.
On the other side, pine trees jut out
Angular, with bark so sharply drawn
It almost feels rough against your hand.
A palanquin is being carried
Up one of those hills Chinese poets
Always complain about, even though
They're never the ones carrying the
Load. On the rise of the next hillside,
A temple hangs in space, partially
Hidden by fog. The official in
The palanquin will rest there for the
Night. The next day, he'll write a poem
In strong, elegant calligraphy
Praising the simple life of the priests.
But, by the time he returns to court,
A new dynasty will be in place,
Mongols will threaten the western lands,
The emperor will have retreated
To the south, and no one will have time
For landscape painting or poetry.

Nothing Dramatic

Of course, it's nothing dramatic. We embrace, and you
Leave to resume your life. I resume mine. Only later
Does this feel difficult. Monday nights especially, when I

Can still smell your skin on the sheets, when I imagine you
Washing in the shower, brushing your teeth, your hair—
That shaking when we hold each other. No matter

How often it happens, it still scares me, how easily
I stop being the person I see in the mirror, the one who
Thinks before speaking, who picks up a glass of wine or

Tastes potatoes and eggs. Grammar doesn't work here.
Desire's without object, or subject. Before words,
Before a self that walks aimlessly, following its shadow

Through suburban streets, before tree roots that crack
The sidewalk with a slow power, before the meal served
On porcelain or the wine that smells of summer

In the thin-rimmed glass, before music or Cezanne's apples,
Icons of saints or Buddhist statues—there was this,
Which couldn't, can't, be expressed. Then, it's Monday.

Your suitcase is stored flat in the trunk of the car, your
Purse on the seat beside you. I stand there,
Watching you leave.

Frank[1]

Eight months later, I think how I saw you last,
Your body limp, your eyes closed by nurses. They

Shuffled me out of the room to prepare your
Corpse for the funeral home. I don't know what

The nurses did, besides washing you one last time.
There was no funeral or minister. Your ashes were sent

To your daughter in Iowa, and I shipped your
Papers to a colleague in Philadelphia. Whenever

We would talk about dying, I'd tell you I expected you to
Live forever. I needed you here to talk about writing, about

A new wine I was sure you'd like, about detective novels
Set in the 1930's, or that recording I found of Etta James

Singing "Nobody's Business." I realize now you'd been
Preparing for death so long that it just seemed normal. You

Lived in an apartment almost devoid of furniture, just
Your desk, your bed, a television, and a chair. The walls

Were almost bare as well. You'd only kept two of Tom's
Paintings, the books you needed to write about the Militia Act

In Pennsylvania, your computer. I've tried to forget those last
Days. They were full of pain and sleep. You were able

To eat one of the madeleines I brought you, and then nothing.
I drive past your apartment complex, the gate that always

Got stuck, the parking spaces that were always full. I can't
Pick you up at 6:30 to go out to eat at a Cuban restaurant or the

---

[1] Francis S. Fox (1925-2017), jazz musician, publisher, historian, author of *Sweet Land of Liberty: The Ordeal of the American Revolution in Northampton County, Pennsylvania*.

Cantonese place you liked, and now there's nothing you
Need at the supermarket. Ximena tells me she's surprised

How I enjoy everything: walking, shopping, going to poetry
Readings in Spanish, where I can only catch a few nouns

As they fly past. Frank, this is something I learned
From you, how you took pleasure in so much. I'm

Surprised sometimes how easy it is to imagine you
Sitting across the table, with a slice of bread and some

Manchego, half a glass of red wine. You pull out a
Shopping bag you've brought with you and pass on a handful

Of books, mysteries you liked or didn't, and an article you've
Found on eighteenth-century judges. You tell me again

About learning to play the trumpet, about troop ships headed
To Europe, and after the war, living in New York. Then,

You take a sip of wine—it's a Ribera I've bought for the occasion—
And you say, "George, that's delicious."

Borges Says Arranging a Library Is an Act of Criticism

After a while, books do what they want.
My Russian poets have scattered. The
French are in the kitchen and elsewhere.
God knows where Dante Alighieri
Ran off to. And, Octavio Paz
Has left my living room to travel
To India, Mexico City,
Or anywhere red bougainvilleas
Climb along mud brick walls. Neruda
Is missing too. He crossed the Andes
In several bad translations. He
Used to live on the third shelf across
From the television. Milosz and
His uncle would hang out there as well,
But now drink slivovitz with Rilke
By the dining room table. Something
About it reminds them of Polish fields
In summer. They've asked Zbigniew Herbert
To join them. Ginsberg, Rexroth, and the
Americans from California
Are still clustered by the sliding glass
Doors that open to the patio,
Stretching their faded spines in sunlight,
Motes of dust. Emily Dickinson
Watches them, smiling, and proceeds to
Crack walnuts with her strong white fingers.

Palimpsest

It's not that I think (if there is an *I* that thinks) that I'm an automaton,
Just that there are all these things we talk about as if they're real
When we've really got no idea. I know that the orchid's deep fuchsia
Catches my eye (sort of). I know what reasoning is, but
I don't know what's doing it. Oh, Descartes! Oh, Hume!
And oh, Bishop Berkeley, I won't forget you either—although
I haven't a clue what's remembering you. Perhaps mind

Is the blackboard in my 2nd grade classroom. My teacher, Miss Davis,
Of unknown age and now in the company of the great philosophers,
Assigned us spelling words, and we'd write them out up there
In chalk and then remove them with erasers made of felt. But,
If you were sitting close enough, you could still see the blurry outlines
Of those scribbles. Very helpful when there was a pop quiz.

By now, my blackboard has been filled and erased so often it's
A dusty palimpsest of letters, numbers, voices, poisonous plants, pet
    dogs, musicians—
Whole encyclopedia volumes with illustrations of hands and lips,
How black eyebrows looked on a moonless night against white skin.
Miss Davis, they're all there, but I can't make sense of them. Or,
I don't know what making sense of them means. My grandfather, whom
    you knew,

Had a storehouse built of thick concrete and stucco set back behind the
    red brick house
Where we lived when he was sick. The storehouse was full of canned
    goods
And light bulbs, toilet paper, whiskey, and cleaning products, bottles of
    wine he'd
Bought or been given. I liked to spend hot afternoons in there where it
    was cool.
But, none of this helps. The canned goods didn't line themselves up
    with the whiskey
And write out equations or compose symphonies. The paper towels
    didn't find themselves
Magnetically drawn to the shoe polish. Metaphors all collapse when
    we talk about whatever it is

That makes metaphors, and a metaphor that contains itself is a
    contradiction in terms.

Then again, we're here, aren't we? The chicken is roasting in the oven.
    I can smell
The sweet onions and the potatoes, the loaf of bread waiting on the
    table.
Somehow, Things happen, and we're part of it. I think of the would-be
    disciple who begged Bodhidharma
To pacify his mind and Bodhidharma's reply: "Show me your mind,
    and I'll pacify it."

Bodhidharma, I can't show you my mind, but knowing that doesn't
    make me enlightened.
There's no gland that squirts out ideas or memories, no throbbing brain
    cells that
One day decided to be a self. We sold my grandfather's house more
    than half a century ago.
The new owners installed a swimming pool in the backyard. I don't
    know
What happened to the storehouse.

Baedeker's Guide to Eternity

Do not look for me under your running shoes
Or in the clouds moving from west to east—
Even though I admit there might be some
Resemblance to my beard and eyebrows in
That puffy one there, stirred by the wind.
Whatever you think, I am not watching you
Like some eternal voyeur hooked up by
Video to your darkest activities. I cannot
Imagine a more boring afterlife. Apologies,
Reader, if that offends your narcissism.
Similarly, do not imagine me conversing
With the illustrious dead. What would we
Really talk about? Aristotle's lost book
On comedy? It's lost. I haven't read it.
Same thing for Bruno Schultz's *Messiah*,
Rotted away or burned somewhere in
Poland. What would I say to Bruno
Except that I'm a fan? Death would be
Like a book-signing party without books.
Milosz (O.V. de Lubicz) says that it
Will be exactly as it is in this life, and
That we must wear our best clothes to go
Into the night. I certainly hope not. I've
Never liked dressing up, or repeating what
I've done before. Sartre imagines that
Hell is other people, and we will suffer
Their obnoxious interference without
Relief: the lady in line at the supermarket
Who wants to write a check but can't find
Her pen, the clever conversationalist at
The cocktail party, the landlord who's given
Up his violin until there's world peace. It's
A Gilbert & Sullivan operetta, never-ending
And sadistic. I think of the times I've been an
Utter fool viewed on a massive screen like
The kissing cam at a baseball game, then
Repeated. Let the record reflect an anxious
Shudder. Like you, I want to think well

Of myself, but fail miserably. Baudelaire
Got it right, *mon hypocrite lecteur*. We will
Find ourselves awake at one in the morning,
Wondering if anyone misses us, or worse.

Crime Scene

The pots from last night's beans have not been washed.
They sit accusingly dirty in the sink,
Accompanied by empty bottles on the counter.
I'd made a roux and slowly stirred it smooth:

Six tablespoons of butter, one of flour,
Leftover wine from the fridge mixed with onions,
And bulk-bought beans I'd soaked and cooked till done—
We ate soft kidneys the color of drying blood.

Apple Harvest

In Pissarro's *Apple Harvest*, the
Tree is no more than a tree, a shape

Angular but made of the same light
As the harvesters, the shadows, the

Dizzying slope of the earth and sky.
The man holding the harvesting stick

Is thin as the tree. Reaching for an
An apple hidden by the leaves, his

Elbow juts out in a sharp bend like
The tree trunk struggling to stand upright

On the turning earth. Two women pick
Up the red fruit, derrieres high in

The air, skirts and aprons brushing the
Ground, folds of thick fabric turned blue in

The shade. But one woman stands staring
Into the branches, her hands touching her

Cheeks and chin, her eyes captured for a
Moment by the apple poised to fall.

Mouths Pressed

Mouths pressed so hard
The next day lips are sore,

We touch for hours before
We fall, convulsed,

Back upon pillows and
Rough sheets, our bodies

Jerking away, toward
Each other, grasping

Our closest parts with slippery
Tongues and lips—

And still I can't define
The word *desire*.

Apology

Male birds, I'm told, will preen their feathers
To make themselves look brighter, larger,

To catch a female's eye. I've wanted to impress
You with poems and sharp observation,

My feathers all the colors of sunlight, orchids
Bowls of fruit, and leather-bound books.

Eventually though, the plumage settles, dull with
Dust, clumped together from inevitable rain.

It's not a pretty sight—like my uncombed hair
When I drag myself out of bed in the morning,

Moving in increments to the kitchen and
The day. But, you've seen that and worse

By now—my pettiness that I despise and then
Despise myself for despising, the piles

Of paper, unopened mail, gathering unattended
On my desk, days I've wasted in my bathrobe,

Reading aimlessly, roaming the supermarket
Like a tourist at the Vatican, replying to

The latest provocation on Facebook, or when
All else fails, walking the dog as he sniffs

The same trees he sniffed the day before.
Even now, I worry I'm trying to glamorize

What's distinctly unglamorous. I don't think
Confession is good for the soul. It only

Tricks you into thinking you're turning the page,
As you read the same passage one more time

Without comprehension. Are apologies
Any better? Probably not, but I'll say it anyway:

I'm sorry I'm not the person I wish I were and
You deserve to have. Do you remember the

Grackle we saw the other day, lucky enough to
Snag two French fries from an unprotected

Plate at an outdoor table? Well, I'm that grackle.

Why Poetry?

What does it matter now? An island
With two hotels and a creaking dock,

Night with the tide rising, cold, unseen,
Up the moonless beach, dinner of bread,

Fish stew, and anis-flavored liquor.
Old men who drink too much, usually

In the same bars, stumbling home to rooms
That smell of things they've lost. A wooden

Shelf beneath a mirror, a bottle
Of hair tonic, a razor, and a

Comb. The filament of a light bulb
Hanging from a wire. A photograph

In a pewter frame, a plate, a knife,
A spoon. To the west, stars drop slowly

Into the sea, small fires extinguished
By the black horizon and the waves.

In the next room, someone is coughing.

In the Ghetto Nuovo

The buildings lean against each other
For support, some peeling paint near where
Two of them meet, like old friends who have

Sunned themselves on better mornings. We
Sit on a bench and eat hard cookies,
Sprinkled with dust. Invisible from

The *campo*, someone is repeating
Morning prayers. Leafless trees shiver.
The wind off the lagoon doesn't stop.

    *

One of the synagogues opens on
A canal. Every Rosh Hashanah,
After the service, bearded men throw

Breadcrumbs out through the windows, and small
Fish come up to the surface to eat
The damp, floating crusts of last year's sins.

    *

Down the Strada Nuova, shoppers buy
Blood oranges from Sicily, tuna
From the Adriatic, and white wine

From Umbria. In the cafés, cups
Of espresso and steamed milk. The bare
Stones and crooked roofs of the ghetto

Are lost behind alleyways and streets.
In the hidden synagogues, polished
Terrazzo floors are cold to the touch.

Nietzsche in Turin, 1889

The horse lying on its side, hind legs shaking—
Above him the whip, the master's claim: justice
Is the advantage of the stronger. The philologist
At first begging the man to stop, then lunging

For the leather whip, his brain filled with animal cries.
The driver shoves him down to the pavement, puzzled
At the interference, not comprehending, the horse's muzzle
Covered in white foam, a thread of blood from the eyes.

He would write, "Ariadne, I love you." He would lapse
Into a silence no one could touch—nothing
Would matter. His moustache would grow long, covering
Lips that no longer spoke. Syphilis.

Vienna 1933-34

"The trouble is—I am an old man— *you do not think it worth your while to love me.*" — Freud to HD[2]

The dog lay by his feet during their sessions,
A lion-like chow with a bad temper, or so he said.
The American insisted on petting her while the shelved
Egyptian gods watched, concerned. She'd been
Known to bite. They spoke of Greece and Pennsylvania,
Of childhood and desire, of the father's distance
And the mother's pain, of the story that repeats
Itself through generations—how what we want
Escapes us. Outside, someone chalked a Star of David
On the walkway. Swastikas were everywhere.
Soon, he would emigrate like the others, or die.
He was old already. His books had been written,
And the ones who had betrayed him didn't matter
Anymore. The ideas they feared now belonged
To others. They were all so frightened of the body
And wanted it to disappear into spirit or myth,
But it refused, oscillating between death and love,
Glimpse of a woman's hand, the wax-formed mask
Of the dead. Staying alive still mattered though,
Just as dreams mattered and silly slips of the tongue.
Affection mattered too—Alcestis making herself
An offering to death to spare an unworthy husband.
But, the objects of love are never worthy, so we give
Ourselves to them to make them capable of loving in return.
That never works either. Hercules only appears in the myths,
Rising from the floorboards to wrestle on our behalf
With death. The beloved will always leave, or we will—
Perhaps with a few words of Greek or a phrase from the Vedas
To justify us. All unnecessary. Just as the *deus ex machina*
Is unnecessary. The affection is what matters, a sprig of white flowers,
Words spoken, that could be spoken to no one else.

---

[2] In 1933, Hilda Doolittle moved to Vienna to work with Freud, attempting to come to terms with her many losses, her overwhelming fear of another war with Germany, and with her sexuality. The quote is from her memoir, *Tribute to Freud*.

A Conversation About Dictators

My son and I were talking about dictators, the sign that
Says "vacancy" hanging on their chests like a medal, a hollow

Space, a room with no furniture, derelict, abandoned. The rest of us
Have no trouble moving in, putting our bed in the corner, our desk

By the window, turning on a light—the emptiness is an invitation
To want things, people, sunlight reflected in water drops, the moon reflected

In the pupil's depths. But, my son and I were talking about dictators,
Men who know there's a country inside them, who can see its borders

Clearly, who set up checkpoints and fences, watchtowers, and machine guns.
The machine guns point out toward everything else, the country on

The other side of the fence, the lights of the city they can see in the dark,
They always have good vision; they eat carrots to see better at night.

Their eyes are always pointed in the same direction as the machine guns.
If anything moves or stirs in the wind, they give instructions to fire, to

Fire the machine guns that point outside the fence. *The tree trunks are
Splintered by bullets. There are no birds left in the forest.* My son asks what

Are they protecting, behind the watchtowers and the fence, and I
Tell him "nothing." They are afraid to look there, frightened by the acres

Of rubble, rough pieces of stone, by the dust and the wind that doesn't
Stop blowing, by the sound that's not a sound. *Think of it like ringing in*

Your ears that never lets up. It's a place where no one speaks. If words

Could be formed there, then that place would be no different from anywhere else,

But it is different. Words never make it past the fence, past the machine guns,
Past a dictator who barely sleeps for fear that dreaming he'll see the space

Inside his chest, the horizon of rubble.

Robert Frost in Key West

The trip down by railroad, surrounded by blue,
The Gulf sheer on one side, the Atlantic braced
Against the sand of the other, two
Wave-rocked giants asleep, the taste

Of salt air on his New England tongue—
He must have dozed, the conductor
Calling, "Key West." He reached for his jacket that hung
On a steel hook. A woman tucked her

Blouse more firmly in her skirt. He thought
How determined virtue is and smiled. Wool can be armor,
But he'd watched her take her hair down from a bun.
Perhaps like him she had a thousand things she ought
To do and wouldn't.
                He settled for whiskey over ice, and like a farmer
Gauging clumps of soil, weighed the unfamiliar tropic sun.

Reading Cesare Pavese in Takee-Outee

The black fan standing in the corner
Sweeps the hot air from one side of the
Room to the other. I sit by the
Door, uncomfortable, waiting for
My General Tso's chicken and rice,
Reading Pavese's "The Country Whore."
A new customer at the counter
Places his order and sits down. It's
A summer evening. The stars are just
Becoming visible in the east.

I think of Pavese wandering
Through the villages outside Turin
Or sipping grappa with one of his
Companions, a woman's delicate
Fingers touching the back of his hand.
I can see the full moon over the
Parking lot, silhouettes of treetops
Darker than the dark sky. Fluorescent
Lights buzz, flicker, over the cooler
Filled with plastic bottles of soda.

What is it I want from Pavese?
Probably the same thing he wanted
From Whitman or Masters, to collapse
Geography and time into words,
To take Brooklyn Ferry across the
Po, to stare at Spoon River from a
Hilltop overlooking Rome. I want
Pavese to take me from table
To table, introducing me to
His friends, party members who defy
Mussolini, exhausted teachers,
Farmworkers who read Dante as they
Cut pieces of soppressata with
A pocket knife, the woman who won't
Wait for him when he's thrown in prison.
What do I want from Pavese? I

Want him not to be dead, not to have
Taken those sleeping pills, gone silent.

The young man from behind the counter
Walks up to me holding a brown bag
Stapled with a menu. General
Tso's chicken and rice, he says. Through the
Paper, I smell fried chicken and sauce.
Cesare, would you share this with me?

Floorboards

It's an old cliché that if you stare
At wood you see shapes, faces. The knots

Become unfocused eyes that observe
Your footsteps without resentment or

Comment, the lines pale rain falling on
A blank ocean, the swirls hands reaching

Toward the sky, holding an offering
In a clumsy bowl. Some days, I see

A map describing a long slope with
Broad chevrons, altitude lines crowding

Closer as you near the peak. Nothing
Grows there, and it's rough against your hand.

If you tell me all this is random
And meaningless, I wouldn't argue—

Just white, fibrous trunks of oak trees cut
To planks and sanded free of splinters,

But how patiently they bear our weight.

Paradox

Zeno's arrow stays in motion. The traffic
However, stops, starts, without getting anywhere.
By the side of the road, Muscovy ducks
Bristle harlequin feathers and peck
At the ground for worms. On the other side
Of the pond, ibises plunge orange beaks into
The tall grass, then fly away. I notice the park
Is flecked with discarded cups and straws, crumpled
Napkins, a plastic bag. A man in shorts and a
Dirty t-shirt sits on a bench, near his bicycle.
Not well-off enough to meditate, he is
Just sitting there, watching the traffic and the
Ducks. Somewhere, a stoplight changes, and
A new set of drivers moves into place. The detritus
Of our life overwhelms, tries to convince us
That we're disposable, that we move on to
New lovers and new lives, and every few years
A new car, that the people who love us move
On as well—move on to what? Zeno's arrow
Hovers in front of me, a signal to turn left. I
Take a deep breath and keep walking. I think
Of Heidegger picking mushrooms in the Black
Forest, of Kant taking his pills for constipation,
And Auden spending his last years in Austria
On a suburban street. Forget the traffic and Zeno.
Tonight, I'll fix a Greek stew with carrots, potatoes, and
Green olives. We'll drink a bottle of wine from
Umbria and read poems till we fall asleep.

"Thus"

Standing alone, it sounds like the name
Of an Egyptian god, one who might
Be worshipped by librarians and
Scholars of ancient languages. But,
It never stands alone. It connects
Propositions of philosophy
To fact, to a dry wrinkled lemon,
A cracked blue porcelain bowl, the light
That angles through the clouds at sunset—
How one thing leads to another thus,
Scratched into papyrus, this notion,
Miraculous, that reason rules the
World, a benevolent king with long
Fingernails and weak eyesight, that time,
His jealous, unforgiving brother
Obeys, albeit reluctantly,
His orders. Thus, was the square of the
Hypotenuse equal to the sum
Of the other sides' squares. Thus, will the
Worm-gnawed flesh fall away from our bones.
Thus, will my last thoughts be of your hand
Touching my arm, your easy laughter.

On a Day in March

It's risky to drive past the airport.
It makes me want to go home and grab

My passport from the bedroom drawer,
Fly to Madrid with Ximena,

See Velázquez's *Head of a Deer*
At the Prado, walk with Eduard in

Barcelona. (He'll show us where he
Buys his scarves.) We could even take a

Train to Paris, circumnavigate
Île de la Cité at night, gargoyles

Staring down at us from cathedral
Walls. But, it's a fantasy. Between

Debts and a leaking roof, travel seems
Unlikely. I'm already teaching

This year at a women's prison. We're
Reading an El Saadawi novel

And maybe Antigone, stories
Of characters who don't compromise—

While my students sit in their baggy
Cotton pants and work shirts, thinking back

To when they were still outside and wore
Whatever they wanted and could go

Wherever their money would take them.
They admire Firdaus who killed her pimp,

And I think they'll feel the same about
Antigone and her loyalty

To her dead brother. Here, everything
Is a compromise. Coming to class

Means risking a strip search. Someone tried
Last week to smuggle in drugs, so guards

Took them all to medical after
A poetry class to pee in a

Plastic cup and be searched. Some—maybe
Abused, angry—don't want to go through

That twice, so they've stayed in the dorms and
Asked other students to bring me their

Papers. Outside the high razor wire
And the gate, I give back the body

Alarm and, after a stare, get back
My driver's license. The sky stretches

Uninterrupted by buildings or
Trees. It's as intensely blue as I've

Ever seen it. A passenger jet
Swings in a wide arc toward the ocean.

Speaking of Love

Speaking of love only gets more difficult.
The words slip out of my hands like a plate I'm

Rinsing and break against the tiles in white
Jagged shards and slivers. They cut my fingers

When I try to pick them up. Even the phrase
"Fall in love" implies an accident, maybe even

A mistake—a tightrope walker slipping, wavering
For how long in the air, as though a breeze

Might set him right again? But it doesn't.
I've never thought our bodies were immortal, and

I'm afraid to calculate my years or yours. That cold
Math belongs to time, not me. I only slide my

Hands along your back, your side, and move
My arm inside your own, my lips pressing against

Your shoulder and your neck. The crowd looks up,
Silent with anticipation. I take a step.

www.ingramcontent.com/pod-product-compliance
Lightning Source LLC
Chambersburg PA
CBHW052103070526
44584CB00017B/2317